Stop Smoking

The Effect Of Smoking On Health And Effective Strategies
To Quit Smoking Promptly

*(Conquer Nicotine Dependency And Effectively Handle
Stress Using Natural Methods)*

ERNEST RAMSAUER

TABLE OF CONTENT

What Are The Primary Challenges Encountered By Individuals Aspiring To Quit? 1

Effective Methods For Cessation Of Smoking Through Natural Means 14

What Would Be The Potential Consequences Of Smoking Cessation? 38

Strategies To Overcome Nicotine Dependence And Achieve Permanent Smoking Cessation 43

Benefits Of Quitting Smoking 71

The Adverse Consequences Arising From Smoking Cessation 77

Seeking Literature 84

An Exclusive Smoking Cessation Program Customized Exclusively For You 97

Herein Lies The Segment That Has Been Eagerly Anticipated: The Benefits. 149

Establishing A Network Of Support 157

What Are The Primary Challenges Encountered By Individuals Aspiring To Quit?

This question is among the least challenging ones posed thus far. Upon thorough examination of their respective cases, it becomes apparent that the issue extends beyond mere physiological factors. This may be attributed to habitual factors (predominantly ingrained attitudes and behaviors) and their individual belief system intertwined with their emotional state.

Nevertheless, when observing from an external perspective, numerous individuals hold the belief that this issue is solely attributable to physical factors. Nonetheless, it is probable that research undertakings and their subsequent findings will contradict this viewpoint. To begin with, the act of resignation can present immense challenges that transcend mere physical capacity. The primary contributor to this phenomenon can largely be attributed to an individual's emotional state. It resembles the act of relinquishing a companion who has remained steadfastly supportive, regardless of one's circumstances, be it at the pinnacle of success or the depths of despair. However, it is crucial to acknowledge that cigarettes are akin to a companion who gradually causes harm to one's well-being. Hence, surmounting the emotional aspect and developing alternative belief systems represent two significant hurdles associated with the cessation of smoking.

There exist individuals who have managed to successfully abstain from their habit following a period of thirty days. Nonetheless, there exist individuals who exhibit a tendency to regress. What are the precise factors contributing to this?

The factors most commonly cited as responsible for the relapse include stress, discomfort, emotional triggers, the consumption of alcoholic beverages, and tobacco smoking. It is disheartening to observe individuals reverting to their previous, detrimental habits shortly after conquering them. However, individuals who have backslid possess the necessary capabilities to revert to a positive and healthy lifestyle. They have previously accomplished this feat, suggesting that they possess the capability to replicate their success once more. It is ultimately their responsibility to either perpetuate the negative habit or completely abstain from it. Once more, it is imperative that individuals acquaint themselves with the potential drawbacks – that is, the anticipated consequences of persisting in smoking and the adverse effects that may arise from this habit.

What are the typical causes of regression?

In precise terms, triggers pertain to exact circumstances that compel an individual to relapse into smoking or anticipate another instance of cigarette consumption. A prime illustration of this phenomenon is being in the presence of individuals who smoke. Certainly, it will compel you to procure an additional stick, and resisting such temptation proves arduous, particularly when those in your vicinity are entirely accepting of it.

Is there a method to ascertain one's probability of attaining success during the cessation endeavor?

There isn't an infallible method to guarantee one's success in quitting. It can be asserted with confidence that it can be categorized into distinct stages. The initial stage of cessation entails self-evaluation. Here, it is imperative that you conduct a careful examination of your smoking habits. Next, you proceed to the phase of building self-assurance subsequent to discerning your specific patterns. Subsequently, you make the necessary arrangements for resignation. It is advisable to refrain from undertaking this decision hastily, particularly if you have not fully determined your readiness for the cessation process. Alternatively, if you approach it hastily, you will encounter a substantial failure. Make the necessary preparations and ensure thorough preparation. It is advisable to allocate ample time for contemplation and consistently consider the enduring advantages that will accrue as a result of this significant life-altering choice.

Resign immediately, and experience a significant increase in your overall happiness within thirty days!

V

itamin

C in

The presence of lemon will significantly alter the flavor of cigarettes, resulting in an unfavorable taste experience. When you get the bad taste, your will no need to smoking for sure. The practice of consuming lemons can aid in the cessation of smoking. Simply slice the lemon into small pieces. When you have the desire to smoke, simply take hold of a piece of lemon and consume it. The presence of the compound found in lemons can assist in diminishing the dependency on nicotine. If you are genuinely intent on smoking, consume the lemon first and proceed with smoking. The presence of vitamin C in lemon causes a reaction with our palate, subsequently altering the flavor of cigarettes in an unfavorable manner.

4

Vernonia cinerea

V

ernonia

cinerea can

Assist you in cessation of smoking. In comparison to alternative smoking cessation treatments, Vernonia cinerea exhibits a greater efficacy in reducing smoking habits than other pharmaceutical smoking control medications. Furthermore, Vernonia cinerea exhibits a comparatively elevated concentration of antioxidants. Consequently, leading to a substantial decrease in the remaining levels of carbon monoxide within the pulmonary system.

The primary factor enabling Vernonia cinerea to assist in smoking cessation is the presence of Potassium nitrate. This subsequently discourages the desire for smoking by inducing a bitter taste sensation on the tongue. Furthermore, white flower grass possesses a blend of nicotine that aids in mitigating the adverse effects associated with cessation efforts. For individuals seeking to cease tobacco consumption through the use of Vernonia cinerea, Vernonia cinerea in the form of tea powder is available for purchase. Due to the inclusion of Vernonia cinerea in the national medicine of Thailand list in 2012.

When consuming tea, it is recommended to utilize a quantity of 2 grams, combined with approximately 120-200 ml of hot water. Allow to steep for a duration of 5-10 minutes, then consume following meals on a frequency of 3-4 times per day. Individuals possessing Vernonia cinerea within their abode may employ desiccated white blossoms, utilizing a quantity of 20 grams per infusion. Subsequently, three glasses of water, approximately 400 milliliters in volume, should be subjected to boiling until reaching the state of ebullition. Filter out. Consume one serving of water, consisting of a single cup, on three separate occasions following meals or whenever the desire to smoke arises. In order to achieve improved outcomes, it is recommended to follow this drinking regimen for a period of approximately two months.

5

Murraya siamensis Craib

The Thai herbs that possess a subtle sweetness. Upon consumption, it elicits a sensory response in our gustatory receptors. After the ingestion of Murraya siamensis Craib leaves, the act of smoking subsequently leads to a discernible deterioration in the flavor profile of cigarettes. Certain individuals may experience symptoms of nausea and subsequently undergo a cessation of smoking. If genuinely resolved to cease smoking, one may consider the utilization of Murraya siamensis Craib leaves, by simply chewing one or two leaves whenever the urge to smoke arises. It necessitates the exercise of patience and reinforcement from both oneself and the individuals in one's vicinity in order to effectively foster the urge to cease smoking.

Effective Methods For Cessation Of Smoking Through Natural Means

1. First, black pepper

Black pepper essential oil has demonstrated potential in reducing cigarette cravings. In a controlled study, participants were instructed to inhale a single drop of pepper oil applied to a tissue for a duration of two minutes whenever they felt hunger.

Based on empirical evidence, it has been determined that the essential oils of angelica and black pepper possess the capability to diminish both the intensity and frequency of cravings, thereby effectively curtailing their severity. While the application of angelica oil demonstrated the ability to increase the duration of time between cravings, black pepper oil exhibited a stronger capability in suppressing them.

The utilization of black pepper oil in aromatherapy may assist in managing cravings; however, additional research is imperative to comprehensively ascertain its full range of potential benefits.

2. Lime Juice, Fresh

Lime juice could serve as a practical and cost-effective alternative to nicotine gum during an effort to cease smoking.

In a particular study, scholars evaluated the quantity of individuals who had successfully discontinued smoking by utilizing lime juice as opposed to individuals who had employed nicotine gum.

Could Potentially Facilitate Smoking Cessation

Based on the findings of the research, individuals who consumed lime juice showed higher rates of smoking cessation compared to those who used nicotine gum after a period of seven days. Nicotine gum exhibited superior efficacy in suppressing the inclination to engage in smoking.

The reason behind the potential ability of lime juice to alleviate cravings remains undisclosed. Scientists have discovered that smokers who lack vitamin C may experience heightened cravings, while the consumption of lime juice can effectively replenish the body's vitamin C levels.

Lime juice also possesses antibacterial properties that aid in bolstering the immune systems of individuals who smoke during the process of recuperation.

3. Changes in Lifestyle

Smoking cessation can be achieved through implementing additional lifestyle modifications including alterations to dietary habits and sleep patterns.

Based on research findings, individuals who engage in smoking behaviors demonstrate a tendency to consume diets that possess a lower degree of nutrient density when compared to those who do not engage in smoking. Consumption of a well-rounded diet can potentially facilitate the cessation of smoking. Please make sure that you are consuming an appropriate amount of water. An excellent measure to proactively manage impulses is to ensure adequate hydration. Exercise restraint in consuming sugar and caffeine. Based on a comprehensive study, it has been established that the consumption of coffee and sugary beverages, including energy drinks, is positively correlated with increased smoking habits.

Research has established a correlation between the adoption of mindfulness techniques, such as meditation, and the cessation of smoking. Furthermore, ensure that you are adequately obtaining sufficient rest and engaging in regular physical activity. Properly attending to your physical well-being and fulfilling these fundamental necessities will have a significant impact on your ability to cease smoking.

4. Hypnotherapy

Hypnotherapy entails a therapeutic approach whereby a patient is induced into a "trance," a notably heightened state of consciousness wherein they gain profound access to their inner thoughts and sensations. A therapist typically assists this type of treatment. It could potentially facilitate the healing process for individuals experiencing trauma and emotional distress. When conducted by a certified practitioner or professional, hypnosis is commonly perceived as a secure form of therapy.

A single randomized experiment has revealed that hypnotherapy demonstrates a slight edge over behavioral counseling in terms of assisting individuals in their efforts to quit smoking. After the cessation period of one year, individuals who underwent hypnotherapy exhibited a success rate of 29% in maintaining their abstinence from smoking. The results exhibited parity, as individuals who underwent counseling to cease smoking achieved a success rate of 28%.

In an alternate inquiry, the effectiveness of nicotine replacement therapies and hypnotherapy were compared. Despite the lack of enhancement in abstinence rates resulting from the combination of the two therapies, the researchers deduced that hypnosis exhibited greater efficacy than NRT in attaining sustained abstinence.

If you harbor reservations regarding the prospect of pursuing hypnotherapy, you may opt for Cognitive Behavioral Therapy (CBT) as an alternative approach. Research has shown that cognitive-behavioral therapy (CBT) can be effective in bolstering an individual's ability to exercise self-restraint against the temptation to smoke.

Strategies for Ceasing the Use of Cannabis

Welcome. This meditative hypnosis serves as a constructive measure towards progress. It signifies your progress along the journey towards improved well-being, increased longevity, and complete liberation from the use of marijuana. By the conclusion of this recording, you will experience a heightened sense of tranquility, enhanced mental clarity, and increased inner strength. Through the harmonization of your subliminal convictions and explicit aspirations, you will experience incremental modifications in your conduct that propel you towards the individual you aspire to become. A completely healthy individual who has permanently abstained from their cannabis dependency.

Let us commence now with a modest respiratory exercise. Commence by diverting your focus away from the external environment, and redirect it inwardly towards your respiratory system. Permit them to gradually and consistently fill, and subsequently exhale when you deem appropriate. It is imperative to ensure that your eyes remain closed while directing your full attention towards your breathing.

Proceed with caution and delicacy. It is recommended to engage in deep breathing exercises only if you experience an inner inclination to do so. Very good. You have been performing admirably up until this point. Please remain in this location temporarily. Facilitate simplicity and ease. This represents the commencement of a enduring metamorphosis.

Continue to inhale and exhale while directing your attention towards the auditory vibrations emanating from my vocalizations. May this serve as your guiding beacon throughout the course of this endeavor. Please revisit it as frequently as necessary to assist you in staying rooted and attentive. As you engage in the act of respiration and attentively perceive sounds, you are gradually experiencing a state of deep relaxation. Your respiration is exhibiting a smooth undulation in your thoracic region, while your cognitive processes are exhibiting a gradual dissipation akin to cumulus formations on a breezy afternoon. Amidst us remains an expanse of unmarred azure heavens, ablaze with the radiant luminescence of awareness.

I kindly request you to envision a scenario where you are gazing towards the vast expanse of the sky. You find yourself reclined on a verdant mound, encircled by resplendent foliage and blooming floral specimens. Perchance, there may be a nearby fountain or lake, whichever suits your fancy. This al fresco space exudes an idyllic ambiance, bearing in mind the subjective nature of such perfection. This is a place where you experience utmost comfort and tranquility, while appreciating the serene magnificence of the surroundings. Direct your attention towards the expanse of the sky, which is remarkably pristine and adorned in a vivid shade of azure. The gentle caress of the sun's rays upon your countenance. You are experiencing a sense of buoyancy, liberation, and optimism. It is an honor to have the opportunity to appreciate such aesthetic splendor, and one fully immerses oneself in every fleeting moment of its presence. Regarding the topic of seconds, I would advise you to observe attentively as a colossal analog clock materializes in the celestial realm. It surpasses the magnitude of an aircraft, even exceeding the considerable dimensions of a structure. The hour and minute hands align vertically, indicating the position of twelve o'clock. We have a particular interest in the abbreviated form. The minute and second hands will adjust and progress in accordance with the time.

Shortly, you will perceive the sound of my finger's rapid closure. And on each instance of performing this action, the hour hand will undergo a clockwise rotation, leading it to the subsequent numeral. Simultaneously, the sun and the sky will undergo subtle alterations, serving as indications of the progressing day. When the hand completes its rotation back to the twelve o'clock position, darkness will descend upon your idyllic location, prompting you to gaze up at the moon and stars instead of the sun. As the countdown toward evening progresses, you will gradually experience a heightened sense of relaxation. Ready? Let's begin.

The hour hand currently rests at the one o'clock position, while the sun has observed a slight spatial displacement in the celestial sphere. We have transitioned into the two o'clock hour, marking the onset of the late afternoon. It is presently 3 o'clock, affording you the pleasure of witnessing the gradual movement of the sun as it ushers in a pleasant decline in temperature. *snap* four o-clock. Very late afternoon now. The sun is commencing its descent, casting a pleasant orange radiance upon the setting at the hour of five. Instantaneously, the clock strikes six, signaling the gradual disappearance of the sun and the advent of a gentle coolness in the surrounding temperature. Click! There are now a total of seven, indicating that the sky has slightly darkened. It is currently eight o'clock in the evening. The evening has arrived, and crickets have commenced their melodious chirping, accompanied by a gentle and refreshing breeze. *snap* nine o clock. As the night falls, your countenance is increasingly unwinding. The time is now 10 o'clock in the evening. You observe a luminous full moon positioned prominently in the expanse above. It is now 11 o'clock, and the night air is pleasantly cool, with stars sparkling in the sky. At long last, the stroke of midnight has arrived.

The atmosphere is serene in your surroundings. As you indulge in the serenading melodies of the twilight hours, your eyes gently shut, embracing the tranquility of the moment. And you are experiencing a profound state of relaxation. Now, permit your inner sight to expand, reminiscent of one's state of dreaming. Visualize yourself situated within a recognizable setting. Perhaps it could be your own residence or the home of an acquaintance. A suitable alternative to express the same idea in a formal tone could be: "A designated area within a workplace facility or the seclusion provided by a personal vehicle." The location and setting you envision should be the optimal environment for engaging in marijuana consumption. It is possible that it is located on your couch following your work hours. Perhaps the situation arises during a gathering amongst friends. Envision yourself within a situation in which you would typically engage in such behavior.

What was your cognitive process during that particular moment? Are you engaging in introspective deliberation or is it an innate, habitual response? The cigarette has been properly prepared and is available to you, prompting a decision that requires your attention. Are you planning to consume it through smoking or do you have alternative plans? Perhaps it is a smoking device, such as a bong or pipe, that you are willing to partake in. Regardless of your preferred approach, envision that. And diligently practice and replicate the mental and emotional process you commonly experience beforehand, when anticipating the impact. Very good.

Let us temporarily halt the scene at this moment. Capture it within the confines of a static image. Please observe the image with utmost attention. Please reflect upon the person you once were. Every day, you express gratitude for the fact that this image belongs to your distant past. You take great satisfaction in discovering wholesome and replenishing methods to unwind and reinvigorate oneself, without relying on the use of cannabis. When you initially started engaging in cannabis consumption, it coincided with a period in your life where you perceived a genuine need for the benefits it purportedly provided. It was an innovative, enjoyable, and highly therapeutic experience at that particular moment. However, in light of your altered perspective, your life has become abundantly rich, to the extent that smoking has become a faded remnant of the past. You possess remarkable resourcefulness, competence, and resilience. You are experiencing contentment and tranquility. There are perpetually available avenues of artistic expression where individuals can discover personal contentment and alleviate stress. Despite any external circumstances, you maintain a state of tranquility and inner balance. Relinquishing cannabis has marked the end of a long-standing companionship.

Instead, healthy cognitive patterns have been established. Your aspirations for your future and the persona you aspire to embody consistently remain present in your consciousness. They engross your thoughts and direct your vitality towards a constructive path. You are in control. Abandoning the use of cannabis permanently proved to be significantly less challenging than initially anticipated. You are thoroughly relishing in the sense of liberation you have acquired. Boredom and cravings have become obsolete. One experiences enhanced cognitive clarity, augmented vitality, and heightened awareness and vitality. You are greatly pleased to have the opportunity to embrace the cherished sense of liberty that has always resided within your aspirations.

Now, let us return to the previous setting. As it undergoes a period of revival, carefully observe the actions carried out by your prior incarnation. They pause briefly, contemplating the cannabis they are about to employ. But they hesitate. One can observe the precise moment when one's previous incarnation reaches a definitive decision. Upon further reflection, they have decided to decline. With an air of tranquility and contentment, they gently set aside the joint or the bong. This decisive moment marked the cessation of your engagement with marijuana, and you have experienced immense satisfaction in making this significant personal choice, firmly resolved to not revisit it.

Gradually let the image of your final moments as a marijuana user dissipate. Experience the satisfaction of achievement. Maintain that feeling of freedom and pride. It is your responsibility to bear them in the future. In a brief span of time, you shall witness my recitation commencing from the number twelve, descending progressively until the number one is reached. Upon encountering the numeral one, your state of alertness shall swiftly be reinstated. You will experience a profound state of tranquility and gain the assurance of successfully attaining your objective. Twelve, eleven, ten, nine, eight, seven, six, five, four, three, two, one." Alternatively, "The countdown commenced, progressing in descending order from twelve to one.

Awaken. Allow me to extend my heartfelt congratulations on your newly acquired state of being free from weed. I express my sincere gratitude to you for joining me in embarking upon this profound journey of meditation.

Experience happiness, ensure your safety, and prioritize your well-being.

What Would Be The Potential Consequences Of Smoking Cessation?

After the cessation of smoking, it takes approximately 20 minutes for the heart rate to return to a standard range, thereby alleviating the condition in which it is excessively elevated.

After a 12-hour period of abstaining from smoking, the concentration of carbon monoxide in your bloodstream will return to a typical range.

Within a period ranging from 2 weeks to 3 months following smoking cessation, one can observe notable improvements in lung function, as well as a substantial decrease in the likelihood of experiencing a myocardial infarction.

Within a time frame of 1 to 9 months after cessation of smoking, individuals will observe a notable decrease in the frequency of coughing episodes and a reduced occurrence of respiratory difficulties.

Following a cessation of smoking for a period of 1 year, your probability of experiencing coronary heart disease reduces by 50% compared to an individual who continues to smoke.

After a cessation period ranging from 5 to 15 years, individuals who have quit smoking exhibit a significantly reduced risk—approximately 50% lower than that of active smokers—of experiencing a stroke. Furthermore, it is worth noting that your likelihood of developing oral cancer, including cancers of the mouth, throat, and esophagus, is reduced by 50% compared to that of a smoker.

Ten years after cessation of smoking, the probability of mortality due to lung cancer is substantially reduced in comparison to that of an individual who continues to smoke.

You are also at a significantly reduced risk of developing bladder cancer compared to a smoker.

In addition, there is a significant reduction in the likelihood of developing cervical, laryngeal, renal, or pancreatic cancer.

After a span of 15 years following smoking cessation, an individual's chances of developing coronary heart disease equal that of an individual who has never smoked.

Once more, it is crucial to highlight that this information ought to be a decisive factor in motivating you to

Break free from your dependence on nicotine and permanently cease the act of smoking.

Strategies To Overcome Nicotine Dependence And Achieve Permanent Smoking Cessation

Getting Started

Overcoming one's addiction to nicotine and permanently quitting the habit of smoking constitutes a formidable endeavor, regardless of whether one is an adolescent who has recently initiated this behavior or an experienced smoker consuming a pack a day. To facilitate the completion of this task, it is necessary for you to acquaint yourself with your available alternatives and engage in mental preparation for the act of quitting. Develop a personalized approach to effectively overcome your addiction, exert authority over your urges, and eliminate the habit permanently.

The Factors That Contribute to the Perceived Challenge of Smoking Cessation

In addition to the physiological dependency, smoking tobacco entails more than just a physical addiction. Additionally, it can be perceived as a psychological propensity. This is attributable to the presence of nicotine in cigarettes. Nicotine affords a transient, highly addictive euphoria. Eliminating your usual nicotine consumption will inevitably result in experiencing physical withdrawal symptoms and cravings. As a result of the psychoactive properties of nicotine in your brain, it is possible that your smoking habit has developed as a coping mechanism for managing stress, depression, anxiety, or sheer monotony.

Furthermore, smoking fulfills an alternate purpose. Certain individuals perceive it as a customary practice that is observed on a regular basis. One might experience the inclination to indulge in a cigarette alongside their morning coffee, amidst their midday respite, whilst partaking in social beverages with acquaintances, or in celebration of the culmination of a challenging day. It is conceivable that individuals within your circle of acquaintances, including friends, family, romantic partners, or colleagues, engage in the act of smoking, and you might perceive smoking as a means of establishing a sense of rapport or connection with them.

To successfully cease smoking permanently, it is imperative to direct your attention towards the addiction's core components and the accompanying behavioral patterns.

Your Personalized Approach to Smoking Cessation

Certain individuals who engage in smoking have demonstrated the capability to quit abruptly through a conscious determination to cease their smoking habits and a resolute refusal to further partake in smoking activities. Other individuals ought to formulate a strategic plan, serving as a roadmap, in order to discontinue the habit of smoking. It can be confidently asserted that this holds true for the majority of individuals who smoke. Unless you possess the immediate capability to renounce smoking, it is highly advisable to formulate a comprehensive plan with the intention of ceasing this habit.

Developing an Effective Plan for Smoking Cessation

"First Stage: Pose the Following Inquiries to Yourself

Take into account the type of smoker that you are. At what precise moment do you experience the desire for a cigarette? What is the root cause of your desire for a cigarette? The objective is to determine which guidance, approaches, or treatments will be the most beneficial in facilitating your cessation of smoking.

Do you experience an inclination for a cigarette during meal periods?

Do you engage in smoking during social gatherings?

What is the frequency or extent of your smoking habits?

Do you have a dependency on tobacco consumption?

Could you consider replacing smoking with the use of a nicotine patch?

Do you experience an elevated desire for cigarettes during periods of stress or depression?

Do you consistently engage in smoking in the presence of specific individuals, during visits to particular locations, or while partaking in specific activities?

Do you have any other dependencies, such as alcohol consumption or engaging in gambling activities, that are closely associated with your smoking habit?

What are the factors that elicit your desire for cigarettes?

To effectively cease smoking, it is imperative to possess awareness of the stimuli that provoke one's desire for cigarettes, in order to subsequently employ the strategies that facilitate the abandonment of this habit. The solutions to the questions stated above will assist you in accomplishing this objective.

Craving Journal

If you continue to encounter challenges in identifying the origins of your cigarette cravings, it may prove advantageous for you to maintain a craving journal. This practice will allow for the acquisition of precise comprehension regarding your habits and stimuli. At what hour do you experience the desire for a cigarette? Please indicate the level of intensity on a numerical scale ranging from 1 to 10, with respect to the strength of your desire or longing. With whom were you in the company of, during the instance when you experienced a strong desire for a cigarette, and what activities were you engaged in at that time? During the period when you experienced the desire for a cigarette, where were you located? What were your emotions like during that period?

Does smoking serve as a means of seeking relief from an unpleasant sensation or from the perception of being ill-equipped to manage such emotions?

Numerous adults engage in smoking as a result of their lack of alternative coping mechanisms for dealing with stress, depression, loneliness, fear, or anxiety. Certain individuals perceive cigarettes as their sole companion during times of melancholy. It is imperative to acknowledge that there exist alternative approaches for addressing these emotions. They exhibit improved health benefits and enhanced efficacy compared to smoke. Engaging in athletic activities, seeking moments of serenity, and practicing mindfulness collectively serve as beneficial and effective means of managing challenging circumstances.

Avoid Smoking Triggers

A significant number of individuals engage in smoking while consuming alcoholic beverages. Henceforth, alcohol may be deemed a catalyst for smoking. One could mitigate this stimulus by opting to consume non-alcoholic beverages as opposed to alcoholic ones.

Other individuals who engage in smoking might also exert pressure on you, thereby stimulating your desire for a cigarette. Kindly inform them that you have firmly resolved to quit the habit and respectfully request that they refrain from smoking in your vicinity. This will facilitate your adherence to your objective.

In conclusion, certain individuals engage in the act of smoking following the conclusion of a meal. If this pertains to your situation, seek out a nutritious substitute to engage in following a meal's conclusion. As an illustration, one could opt to consume a serving of fruit or engage in a leisurely stroll subsequent to a meal, rather than partaking in the act of smoking.

It is advisable to disassociate smoking from any other addictions you may have, if applicable, to facilitate the process of quitting smoking. If you engage in gambling activities, refrain from smoking during such endeavors. Do something healthier instead.

Second Step: Select a Specific Date for Smoking Cessation

Select a suitable date in the near future when you will cease the habit of smoking.

Allocate a sufficient amount of time for your mental adaptation to the notion of permanently relinquishing smoking. In the event that you have successfully identified a particular time or location during which you engage in smoking, please take this into consideration when selecting an appropriate date to cease this habit. As an illustration, in the event that you have a recurring habit of smoking during weekends when you gather with a particular circle of acquaintances, abstain from smoking on a weekday instead. Allocate a conclusive weekend wherein you shall grant yourself permission to cease the habit of smoking, and subsequently renounce it upon the conclusion of said weekend. By employing this approach, you will be granted an entire workweek during which you may acclimate to the alteration.

On the other hand, if you have a tendency to smoke during work hours, consider refraining from doing so during the weekend.

Step Three: Inform Your Acquaintances and Professional Connections About Your Decision to Quit Smoking

Communicate to these individuals that you have committed to permanently cease smoking, and elucidate the significance of their support, comprehension, and motivation during this period. If you happen to have a companion who shares your desire to quit smoking, collaborate! Develop a strategic approach collectively and provide mutual support to overcome this addictive behavior. You may also hold each other responsible for your actions and pursue together the goal of cessation.

Step Four: Develop a comprehensive plan for effectively managing the obstacles that are likely to arise during the process of smoking cessation.

Research findings indicate that individuals who cease smoking often experience a relapse, resuming smoking within three months of their initial cessation date. One can prevent relapses by implementing strategies to address various challenges, such as nicotine cravings, emotional disturbances including anger, frustration, irritability, depression, and the potential for weight gain.

Managing Your Nicotine Cravings

You are inevitably going to encounter nicotine cravings. The reason for this is that, when you were smoking, your body became accustomed to a specific level of nicotine. The nicotine concentration in your system was contingent upon factors such as the quantity and type of tobacco you consumed, as well as the extent to which you deeply inhaled the tobacco. Upon cessation, your physical being will solely yearn for nicotine. Additionally, it is possible to experience a desire for nicotine due to the observation of others engaging in smoking behavior. Cravings are not a product of your imagination but rather a genuine phenomenon. They have the potential to induce alterations in your emotional state, elevate your heart rate, and raise your blood pressure. Desires will ebb and flow. They are not permanent; a desire usually emerges within one to two hours after smoking the last cigarette, escalates to its peak for approximately one week, and persists for a duration of one to two months. One can effectively manage their cravings by reminding oneself that they are transient in nature. One can also effectively mitigate cravings by refraining from associating with individuals, locations, or activities that are linked to smoking. If your longing for smoking stems from the ritualistic aspect or the physical sensation of manipulating objects between your fingers, you might find it worthwhile to seek out a more wholesome alternative ritual, such as the act of peeling and consuming carrots. Moreover, the consumption of carrots or any other nutritious and innocuous alternative has the potential to alleviate the urge to smoke by occupying the oral cavity. It is advisable to consult your physician regarding potential pharmaceutical options or alternative products that can serve as nicotine substitutes.

Managing Your Anger, Frustration, and Irritability

Ceasing the habit of smoking is inclined to result in altered mood and heightened irritability. One may experience a decrease in their tolerance for task completion compared to their usual level. You may find yourself with a diminished tolerance for individuals and hence may become inclined to engage in disputes with them. Research findings have demonstrated that individuals who cease smoking often experience emotions characterized by anger, frustration, and irritability. These emotions often exhibit pronounced intensity one week following smoking cessation and may persist for a duration of up to one month. One may potentially manage these emotions by affirming that they are merely transient in nature. Possibly, you may consider adopting a physical pursuit to engage in during moments of emotional overload. Engaging in a leisurely stroll or partaking in a workout at the fitness center might greatly assist you. Additionally, given that the consumption of caffeine has the potential to initiate such sensations, it would be advisable to consider decreasing the quantity of caffeine you consume. Caffeine can be found in coffee, tea, and carbonated beverages. You may wish to consider engaging in relaxation techniques, such as practicing mediation or yoga. Even indulging in a lengthy, warm bath may provide assistance. Lastly, it is important to bear in mind that your healthcare provider can also provide guidance on effectively managing these emotions.

Managing and mitigating your anxiety

It is probable that feelings of anxiety will manifest within a 24-hour timeframe subsequent to the cessation of smoking. Additionally, it is possible that you may experience sensations of tension in the muscles located in your neck and shoulders. Research has demonstrated that anxiety emerges as one of the prevailing emotions experienced as a consequence of quitting smoking, with a potential duration of up to a fortnight. Managing anxiety becomes more feasible when one remembers that it is temporary and will eventually subside. It would be advisable to allocate a portion of your daily schedule towards personal relaxation. Allocate sixty minutes each day to relax and attend to any feelings of anxiety. You might consider engaging in a light jogging routine, indulging in spa treatments, or reducing your caffeine intake in order to manage the situation more effectively. Furthermore, your physician can offer guidance regarding pharmaceutical options and nicotine substitution aids.

Effectively Managing Your Depression

Experiencing depressive feelings subsequent to smoking cessation is a fairly typical occurrence.

With that being said, it is important to note that the occurrence of major depression is uncommon among former smokers with no prior history of depression.

Conversely, individuals with a prior history of depression may experience more pronounced withdrawal symptoms compared to individuals with no prior history of depression. Individuals with a documented history of depression may experience an exacerbation of depressive symptoms subsequent to smoking cessation, particularly if they undergo a new, notable episode of depression upon quitting.

A considerable number of individuals who have quit smoking experience a strong desire to smoke when they are experiencing feelings of depression. You can effectively manage this desire by contacting a companion and engaging in a shared activity, such as attending a film screening in a smoke-free setting. This would aid in abstaining from smoking, attending a concert, or engaging in any other enjoyable endeavor. Make an effort to comprehend the underlying reasons for your experience of depression. Should you find yourself fatigued, famished, or disinterested, discovering resolutions for these concerns may effectively alleviate both your state of depression and your longing for cigarettes. Additionally, one may alleviate or eradicate their depression through engagement in a physical activity or sport. Physical activity stimulates the release of endorphins, which contribute to an elevation in one's emotional state. Hence, it is advisable to pursue a physical activity if one is experiencing feelings of depression. Furthermore, it is advisable to document the factors contributing to your depression and subsequently devise effective strategies to address and resolve these issues.

Preventing Weight Gain

After relinquishing the habit of smoking, a substantial number of individuals experience weight gain. This is due to their tendency to indulge in food whenever they experience a craving for a cigarette, which is an unhealthy practice. A significant proportion of individuals who cease smoking tend to experience an average weight gain of approximately 10 pounds. Certain individuals may encounter challenges when it comes to accepting this concept. Nevertheless, it is crucial to emphasize that prioritizing weight gain, albeit to a modest extent, is more beneficial for one's well-being than persisting with smoking and maintaining a slightly lower body weight. If you have any concerns regarding the possibility of weight gain, it would be advisable for you to consult with a medical professional to inquire about the medication known as 'bupropion'. This medication has demonstrated efficacy in mitigating the potential for weight gain.

Alternative products have the potential to mitigate the effects of weight gain. Some examples of such products encompass nicotine gum and lozenges. It is important to bear in mind that engaging in physical exercise and maintaining a nutritious diet also serves as a dependable approach to achieving weight loss goals. If one observes a significant increase in weight, it would be prudent to consider enrolling in a fitness facility. Engage in physical exercise at a minimum frequency of once every week. Eliminate sugar and alcohol from your dietary intake, as their consumption has the potential to contribute significantly to weight gain. This will undoubtedly assist you in avoiding weight gain.

Step Five: Dispose of any cigarettes that might be present in your vehicle, residence, and place of employment.

Dispose of all the remaining cigarettes in your possession. Dispose of any additional smoking utensils, including lighters and ash trays. Please proceed with laundering your garments and thoroughly eliminate any residual cigarette odors within your residence, vehicle, and place of employment. This will hinder your thoughts of cigarettes, consequently reducing the probability of cravings. Enforce a prohibition on smoking within the confines of your vehicle, residence, and place of employment as well. This is due to the possibility of succumbing to the temptation of resuming smoking in the presence of someone else who is smoking.

Step Six: Notify your physician of your decision to quit smoking.

Your healthcare professional has the ability to provide encouragement and assistance in your commitment to overcome this addiction. For instance, a medical professional can proactively administer pharmaceuticals to alleviate withdrawal symptoms and proffer strategies to effectively manage the cessation of smoking. Furthermore, a physician can also serve as a crucial source of guidance, emphasizing the multitude of health advantages associated with permanently abstaining from smoking. By drawing attention to the long-term objective and fostering a sense of pride in one's actions, the doctor aids in maintaining focus and determination.

Benefits Of Quitting Smoking

Cessation of tobacco use has the potential to significantly impact both one's physical well-being and overall quality of life. It is never too late to discontinue smoking in order to greatly enhance your well-being. For instance, if one were to cease smoking during middle age, prior to the onset of cancer or any other grave ailments, one significantly mitigates the substantial mortality risk associated with smoking. Assistance can be provided to individuals who encounter difficulties in ceasing their smoking habit.

The benefits start immediately.

By relinquishing your age, you decrease the likelihood of contracting severe illnesses. Fortunately, the sooner you cease, the greater the mitigation of your risk. In fact, researchers have uncovered that if an individual ceases the habit of smoking prior to the age of 50, their probability of mortality is significantly diminished to a level comparable to that of a non-smoker. Even in the event of surrendering after the age of 60, the risk of mortality at any given age decreases by approximately 39% in comparison to individuals who continue to engage in smoking.

By discontinuing the habit of smoking, you will:

Minimize the risk of succumbing to smoking-related ailments, including but not limited to cardiovascular disorders, malignant neoplasms, chronic obstructive pulmonary disease (COPD), and peripheral vascular disease.

Mitigate the risk of acquiring various other conditions that, while not necessarily serious, can give rise to unwanted complications. As an illustration, some notable health conditions that may arise include: erectile dysfunction (difficulties with achieving and maintaining an erection), issues with reproductive capabilities, optic neuropathy (a disorder that impacts the ocular nerve), cataracts, macular degeneration (deterioration of tissue at the back of the eye), psoriasis, periodontal disease, tooth loss, osteoporosis, and Raynaud's phenomenon (where fingers become pale or blue when exposed to cold temperatures).

Minimize the risk of pregnancy complications for expecting individuals.

If you have been a regular smoker since your adolescent or early adult years:.

If one ceases the habit of smoking prior to reaching approximately 35 years of age, their lifespan experiences only a marginal reduction, as their life expectancy will be almost equivalent to that of individuals who have abstained from smoking entirely.

If an individual ceases smoking prior to the age of 50, the likelihood of succumbing to smoking-related ailments is significantly reduced by 50%.

However, it is never too late to discontinue the habit of smoking in order to attain health benefits. Even if you currently have actually COPD or cardiovascular disease, your outlook (prognosis) is much boosted if you stop smoking.

Additional advantages associated with cessation of smoking.

These consist of:.

Your breath will no longer carry the scent of tobacco that has gone stale.

The lingering odor of stagnant tobacco will also dissipate from your garments, tresses, and abode.

Both the flavors and aromas of food and beverages are heightened.

Significantly improved insurance plan rates.

You are highly likely to experience a genuine sense of self-satisfaction.

The Adverse Consequences Arising From Smoking Cessation

It is probable that you are currently holding this book due to the guarantee presented on its cover, which assures an instruction on how to stop smoking without experiencing any adverse effects. I am determined to fulfill that commitment, commencing from Chapter Five. Nevertheless, in order to adequately equip you for the cessation of smoking, it is imperative that you possess a comprehensive understanding of the aforementioned side effects and the underlying reasons for their manifestation during the cessation process. Let us commence by examining the typical adverse effects associated with smoking cessation and exploring the underlying causes thereof.

Depression: Individuals who make an attempt to cease smoking frequently experience a profound state of melancholy. The rationale behind this is relatively straightforward. When the customary gratification of your body, namely the discharge of dopamine and other neurotransmitters, is withheld, your body perceives a deficiency of essential elements for its sustenance. As an illustration, let us ponder the potential outcome if one were to provide a young child with a piece of confectionery every hour throughout the course of an entire year. Should you abruptly cease the provision of candy to him, he would manifest a multitude of the aforementioned symptoms, including the onset of profound melancholy. The occurrence of depression stems from the body's preference for the sensory experience induced by smoking, coupled with a subsequent longing for that sensation in its absence.

Heightened Restlessness & Impaired Focus: In the absence of nicotine, the body undergoes a state of heightened anxiety and decreased ability to concentrate. Consider the scenario where you arrive at your residence to find your family famished, having not consumed any food throughout the entirety of the day. Upon their hopeful inquiry about dinner, you deliver the unfortunate news that you will not be preparing a meal, asserting that they must manage with whatever sustenance they can locate. Without delay, your spouse and children would promptly enter an analogous state of distress, diligently rummaging through the cupboards in an attempt to locate a conveniently prepared meal, or meticulously scouring the phone directory for a restaurant's delivery options. Your physical condition remains unchanged. It commences its search for means by which it can procure the customary supply of nicotine.

Excessive Irritability, Anger & Frustration: The cause of this irritability is equally evident. When the absence of the anticipated nicotine is experienced, various physiological, psychological, and emotional alterations manifest. Our physical condition strongly urges us to supply it with nicotine, while we are exerting maximum effort to resist yielding. This would elicit feelings of irritability and sullenness in individuals.

Physical Sensations Linked to Cessation: Individuals may encounter physical manifestations, including disturbed sleep patterns or unsettling dreams, tingling sensations in the limbs, feelings of nausea, and sweating, as well as exhibiting cold symptoms such as coughing. This can be attributed to the body experiencing nicotine withdrawal, along with the body's recognition of the harmful properties of the substance and its subsequent efforts to eliminate it, often resulting in coughing as a natural response. Subsequently, we will discuss strategies to address these symptoms. However, it is important to remember that they will intensify approximately 48 hours following the cessation of smoking, after which they will become more tolerable.

Excessive weight gain: This constitutes a prominent justification cited by individuals when questioned about their reluctance to cease smoking. Gaining an additional ten or twenty pounds is not an uncommon occurrence when ceasing the habit of smoking. Fortunately, this issue can be effectively addressed, and we will explore the corresponding strategies in Chapters Five and Six. In terms of comprehending the underlying cause, it is important to bear in mind that your body is seeking to compensate for the absence of nicotine by readily substituting it with food. Consuming food elicits the activation of similar neurotransmitters as nicotine, serving as a means for the body to endeavor towards its earlier homeostatic state.

Seeking Literature

Dedicate ample time to acquiring knowledge, through diligent study. Literature, written exercises, and various educational resources serve as indispensable instruments for effectuating transformations in one's habits. There exists a vast multitude of perspectives pertaining to this subject matter, all of which are available to assist you in undergoing a transformation in your perspectives. We will engage in discourse pertaining to various literary genres and additional bodies of work, thereby enabling you to cultivate literature for personal growth.

Literature pertaining to smoking cessation can encompass a multitude of formats. Any literary publications, including but not limited to books, magazines, and pamphlets. Literature pertaining to wellness, personal development, inspiration, dependence, or any subject with a positive stance, has the ability to not only educate us but also foster a mindset that urges cessation.

Suggestions

I would recommend adopting the approach of envisioning the author's literature as if it were tailored exclusively for your benefit when engaging with it. You are the sole individual. However, be cautious. The author might be addressing you individually in this hypothetical scenario, but similar to engaging with the contents of this book or conversing with any ordinary individual in society, it is not obligatory for you to consider everything written as an unquestionable doctrine that demands adherence. Please, select necessary items and leave any remaining items. If it fails to align with a viable option for you, do not exert undue pressure. Unless the matter at hand pertains to something beneficial for your well-being, such as adhering to a dietary regimen, and you engage in self-denial because it contradicts your personal desires. Therefore, undertake the demanding task as you are already aware of its beneficial effects on your well-being.

Types of Books

Allow me to discuss a range of book genres that I would recommend to foster the enrichment of your exceptionally astute and magnificent intellect.

Motivation and Inspiration

Allow us to commence by selecting self-help books that instill motivation and inspiration. These books invigorate me. I am drawn to the introspective nature they inspire as I engage with their content. I have frequently pondered the idea of pursuing a career as a motivational speaker in the future; however, my current level of motivation does not align with this aspiration.

Due to the inherent difficulties associated with quitting smoking, I would like to suggest a highly commendable book authored by William H. I made use of the audio rendition of Danforth's thought-provoking work, 'I Dare You!,' as it imparted a greater sense of potency to this remarkable literary composition.

"I challenge you!" brings it back to the olden days. Danforth penned it during the 1930s. It fosters self-motivation and challenges individuals to consistently strive for personal growth and surpass their own limits. The book is remarkable in its relevance and applicability to contemporary society. The book provides a comprehensive perspective on the importance of self-improvement and the pursuit of momentum in one's life.

Other Addiction Books

Perusing a literature on addiction would prove to be an enriching experience, enabling one to delve into the intricacies of cerebral functioning. Understanding the origin of emotions and the underlying causes of your behavior will aid in cultivating mindfulness towards your disordered cognitive patterns. Acquiring knowledge about addiction will provide you with a significantly altered viewpoint as to the reasons behind our persistence in engaging in undesirable behaviors.

Journal- What?

In addition to reading, writing would serve as a valuable complement to your collection of books. A journal is regarded as one of the most impactful instruments an individual can possess when endeavoring to overcome addiction. Maintaining a personal journal provides an effective means to transcribe various thoughts onto paper, thereby alleviating the burden on one's mind. On certain occasions, when I articulate my thoughts or emotions in writing, I endeavor to gain a different perspective on them. I reflect upon the imprudence of allowing myself to be consumed by such an untainted thought or emotion. Should I provide any valuable information, I would emphasize the significance of maintaining a means of expression, such as maintaining a personal journal. When encountering challenging circumstances, one will have the capacity to document their reflections.

Gratitude List

Furthermore, apart from the practice of journaling, compiling a gratitude list serves as an excellent alternative method for documenting your thoughts, albeit with a slightly distinct perspective. I have recently resumed the practice of maintaining a gratitude list. Although it may seem foolish and unproductive, I have remained committed to the practice of maintaining gratitude lists for many years. Nevertheless, I failed to uphold the principles I advocated, and most recently succumbed to the same behavior during a period of low morale. I experienced profound feelings of despair and a pervasive sense of hopelessness. I made the choice to compile a catalogue consisting of ten elements that evoke a sense of gratitude within me, reflecting upon my life experiences. I commenced by focusing on the most notable aspects, encompassing familial and social connections, ultimately culminating in an examination of even the most insignificant elements, such as a single blade of grass. I assure you, it may surprise you...a single blade of grass! It elicited mirth from me, which aided in detaching myself from my thoughts. I have been engaging in this activity consistently for a period of one month, every morning prior to commencing my daily tasks.

Audiobooks

To conclude the compilation of my recommendations pertaining to literature, it is my suggestion that you partake in the activity of indulging in audiobooks. Audiobooks evoke an excessive sense of enthusiasm within me. I am willing to exhaust all efforts in order to procure this book in an audio format. I hold the view that one of the most noteworthy factors influencing my desire for personal growth and development was the consumption of audiobooks. I commenced my journey by procuring antiquated detective radio series, after which I developed an insatiable penchant for immersing myself in a wide array of audiobooks. Encouragement, stimulation, guidance, financial guidance, literature by James Patterson, neural science

I craved various things, be it subconscious thoughts or addictive substances, I desired them all. I would listen to them during car rides, prior to retiring for the night, during leisurely moments outdoors, while strolling, during work hours at the workplace, and in any environment where I could engage without causing inconvenience to others. Please examine any of the aforementioned books. Please consider availing yourself of the opportunity to participate in a complimentary trial of

Audible. Please visit the website www.audible.com/Free-Trial[3]

Summary

In conclusion, literature and education serve as invaluable instruments in embarking upon the endeavor of overcoming the pernicious addiction of smoking. Seek out a diverse range of categories that ignite your interest. A wide range of sources can contribute to an understanding of oneself and the most effective approaches to cessation of smoking. Approach the reading material with the perspective that it has been tailored specifically for your benefit, extracting the information that is most relevant and useful to you. Allow someone else, who is dissimilar to yourself, to handle the remaining tasks. Please remember to attempt composing on your own. Engaging in uninhibited stream of consciousness writing while incorporating expressions of gratitude can serve as a liberating endeavor. Finally, try an audiobook. Make it a habit to regularly engage with them whenever you have a yearning for additional knowledge or entertainment. Absorb all the information across various domains and cultivate a mindset that allows for intellectual growth by broadening your mental horizons.

An Exclusive Smoking Cessation Program Customized Exclusively For You

There exist numerous methods to cease smoking; however, once the decision is made, one ought to acknowledge that it entails a significant alteration in one's lifestyle. It entails a considerable undertaking, necessitating the creation of a meticulous, coherent, and systematic blueprint. A well-devised strategy should encompass two primary considerations: the immediate objective of ceasing smoking and the enduring transformation of safeguarding against missteps and relapses. Allow me to present you with a step-by-step guide on commencing and establishing your personal 'Smoking Cessation Program'.

PHASE 1: INITIATING IT PROPERLY

Identifying your 'WHYs'

Allocate a brief period to contemplate upon your life in the context of being a smoker. Pose the question to oneself, "For what reason am I engaging in the act of smoking?" What benefits does it provide me with? What are the potential benefits or rewards that I would receive if I cease the current activity? "Am I adequately prepared to emancipate myself from smoking permanently?" The process of quitting smoking becomes more manageable as one begins to foster honesty with oneself.

The initial step is to ascertain the rationale underlying your desire to cease. These inquiries will act as your driving force, throughout the entire process of ceasing. Obtain a writing instrument and a sheet of paper, and meticulously transcribe your motivations for desiring to cease your current endeavors. Ensure that this list is readily accessible by storing it in your wallet, purse, or another convenient location where it can be easily retrieved in moments of temptation to smoke. Presented below are several justifications that have been employed by certain smokers in order to cultivate the impetus to cease their smoking habits. It is plausible that these rationales could potentially resonate with you as well, should you choose to adopt them.

I anticipate an improvement in my physical wellbeing." "I expect a favorable enhancement to my state of health." "I envisage a positive change in my overall wellness." "I project an amelioration in my bodily condition.

- In what manner would it be more advantageous? Please compile a catalogue of the illnesses that can be prevented by embracing a smoke-free lifestyle, along with the additional positive impacts on health that arise from cessation.

I am capable of increasing my savings.

May I inquire about the extent of your potential savings? Please record your computation along with any potential purchases that can be made with the resulting sum.

My family and friends will derive great pleasure from this." "My family and friends will find joy in this." "This news will bring delight to my family and friends." "Those dear to me will experience immense happiness.

- What is the reason for their happiness? - What is the cause for their happiness? - What is the underlying factor contributing to their happiness? To what extent do you prioritize their well-being and contentment?

I will experience a heightened sense of self-worth.

- How would discontinuing the habit of smoking enhance your well-being? - In what manner would ceasing the act of smoking contribute to your overall improvement? - What benefits would you gain from refraining from smoking?

I am committed to setting a positive example for my children.

I will have the capability to engage in additional physical activity.

Smoke will not leave its odor on my breath, clothes, or hair.

Not only will my family members and friends also experience improved health.

I will experience a sense of autonomy and empowerment in regards to my decision-making and overall life circumstances.

I, along with others, shall take pride in myself.

Inaugural Measures/Pointers for the Implementation of an Ecologically Conscious 'Cessation of Smoking Initiative'

Once you have firmly ingrained the idea of ceasing smoking in your mind and have documented your motivations and justifications for quitting, it marks the commencement of the actual endeavor. Below are a few guidelines on how to commence in a proper manner:

Establish a designated termination date

- Kindly select a date within the upcoming fortnight during which you will abstain entirely from smoking.

Gradually reduce your cigarette intake.

In anticipation of your designated cessation date, gradually decrease the quantity of cigarettes you consume. If you currently consume two packs of cigarettes daily, reduce your intake to just one pack.

Please make a notation of your activity, the time of day, and the severity of your craving at the time of smoking. The purpose of this is to ascertain the factors that cause you to smoke.

Inform your family and acquaintances of your intention to cease the habit of smoking.

- Inform them of your resolute intention to cease the activity and express your need for their assistance and motivation.

- Additionally, one may seek out a cessation partner, an individual who shares a firm commitment to quitting.

Acquire awareness of the obstacles you will encounter

- Recognize that you will inevitably experience withdrawal symptoms and intense cravings. - Bear in mind that enduring withdrawal symptoms and intense cravings will be part of the process. - It is important to realize that you will encounter withdrawal symptoms and powerful cravings.

Make it a priority to acquire the necessary knowledge and skills to effectively counteract these challenges well in advance of encountering them.

Eliminate the presence of cigarettes in your private residence and professional environment.

Ensure that you dispose of your cigarettes, lighters, and ashtrays several days prior to your designated quit date.

- Launder your garments, linens, and other articles that may carry a residual cigarette odor.

Talk to your doctor

- Consult with your healthcare provider regarding your intention to cease. He/she has the ability to recommend and administer medications or substitution treatments that can assist you in managing your urges.

Purchase a significant quantity of oral replacements.

- Ensure that you have readily available options such as sugar-free gum, mints, cinnamon sticks, coffee stirrers, mint-infused toothpicks, carrot sticks, and straws.

These oral alternatives offer effective assistance in resisting tobacco temptations during moments of smoking cravings.

Knowing your Smoking Triggers

During the period of one week or longer in which you have reduced your cigarette intake, it is possible that you have observed occasions where your desire for cigarettes surpassed the ordinary level. These are commonly referred to as your 'smoking cues.' Smoking triggers encompass stimuli, individuals, or periods during the day when one experiences heightened cravings for smoking. The process of identifying these triggers will assist you in effectively managing them upon complete cessation of smoking.

In order to ascertain their presence, it may be prudent to maintain a log detailing one's cravings. Amidst episodes of intense longing, it is advised to meticulously document the responses to the following inquiries:

May I inquire as to the present time?

On a scale of 1 to 10, how strong is your desire?

What is your current activity?

Where are you?

Who are you with?

What do you feel?

Please make note of the locations, timings, circumstances, individuals, and emotional states that predominantly trigger your cravings. The following are common stimuli that often lead to smoking and strategies to mitigate their impact:

Alcohol

If you have a tendency to engage in smoking while consuming alcohol, consider choosing non-alcoholic beverages as an alternative. You may consider consumption of tea, juice, or a generous amount of water as potential options.

Alternatively, you may opt to consume beverages in a setting where the act of smoking is not permitted. It is advisable to modify your daily schedule and refrain from visiting drinking establishments during the initial week after giving up alcohol.

Other smokers

- Should you have acquaintances or relatives who engage in smoking, inform them of your intention to cease this habit.

When in the company of your smoker social circle, endeavor to engage in alternative activities. You may opt to indulge in chewing gum or any alternative until your urge subsides.

- Additionally, it would be beneficial to associate yourself with individuals who do not engage in smoking or have successfully quit, as their presence will provide you with the necessary encouragement and support in your endeavor to quit smoking.

Coffee breaks

- Several individuals who engage in tobacco consumption partake in smoking activities while taking coffee breaks. During the initial phase following the determination to cease, it may be wise to refrain from consuming coffee as well.

If it is unavoidable to consume coffee, seek out alternatives.

After a meal

- A frequent smoking cue can also arise subsequent to a meal. The initial period will pose significant challenges, therefore it is imperative for you to select an alternative course of action that you can ultimately accept.

Possible alternative in a formal tone: - It may consist of fruit, a nutritious dessert, chocolate, or gum.

Boredom

If one finds themselves smoking out of idleness, it would be beneficial to explore alternative pastimes.

- One can engage in the activity of walking or pursue personal hobbies, while consciously avoiding any distractions that may divert attention from the cravings.

When faced with a smoking stimulus, make a concerted effort to redirect your focus towards alternative activities. Certain emotions and circumstances may be inevitable, yet it is imperative to bear in mind that ultimately, you possess dominion over your decisions and choices. When experiencing a longing, it is advised to refrain from igniting any form of indulgence. Desires, fleeting in nature, endure merely for a brief period of time. As you persevere through the resistance of each such yearning, bear in mind that you are gradually progressing towards a life liberated from the shackles of nicotine.

On your Quit Day:

Smoking is strictly prohibited, including the consumption of even a single cigarette.

Consume a copious amount of liquids.

Steer clear of circumstances that may incite your desire to smoke.

Engage in physical activities

Peruse informative literature on the subject of smoking cessation.

Avoid alcoholic drinks.

Phase 2: Managing the Effects of Withdrawal Symptoms

Upon reaching your designated cessation date, you will promptly experience symptoms of withdrawal. They will manifest themselves within one hour of your final cigarette and reach their maximum intensity within a span of 2-3 days. It is anticipated that these symptoms will manifest themselves as your body undergoes nicotine withdrawal. The duration of the symptoms may vary among individuals, however, it typically persists for a period ranging from several days to a few weeks.

These symptoms are indeed discomforting, yet it is important to comprehend that they are merely transitory in nature. The improvement of their condition will ultimately ensue after the complete elimination of toxins from their body. In the interim, seek support and understanding from your loved ones as you navigate through the challenges of nicotine withdrawal.

Below are the typical signs of withdrawal and strategies for managing them:

Cigarette cravings

- Duration: The intensity of cravings persists strongly during the initial fortnight and may endure for an extended period of time.

- Coping strategy: Redirect your focus, utilize oral alternatives

Insomnia

- Timeframe: 14-28 days

- Coping strategy: Refrain from consuming coffee after 6 PM; engage in physical exercise two hours prior to sleep, practice yoga, and employ other relaxation methods.

Coughing

- Length of time: 1 to 4 weeks

- Coping strategy: Consider it a normal part of the lung regeneration process, ensure adequate hydration, and seek medical guidance for prescribed cough remedies.

Irritability, anxiety, depression

- Estimated time frame: 2-4 weeks

- Coping Mechanism: Engage in meaningful dialogue with individuals in your support network, indulge in warm baths, partake in gentle and calming physical activities, refrain from consuming caffeinated beverages.

Restlessness and fatigue

- Timeframe: 14-28 days

- Coping strategy: Engage in occasional periods of sleep, partake in activities that promote relaxation, avoid excessive exertion, and prioritize rest if necessary.

Increase in appetite

- Timeframe: 1 to 2 months

- Coping strategy: Consume low-calorie food and maintain proper hydration, engage in consistent physical exercise - Coping technique: Incorporate a diet of low-calorie foods and ensure adequate hydration, partake in regular physical activity - Coping method: Adopt a dietary regimen consisting of low-calorie options and stay well-hydrated, engage in frequent physical exercise.

STAGE 3: MANAGING CRAVINGS

The process of reducing your cigarette consumption might have presented challenges, but it is important to prepare yourself for the intense cravings that are likely to persist during the initial two-week period of quitting. Outlined below are a few strategies to aptly control the inclination to engage in smoking behavior.

Divert your attention

- Engage in physical activities: Perform tasks around the house, engage in physical exercise, take a leisurely stroll, indulge in personal grooming, initiate a phone call with a friend, or visit a location that sparks excitement.

- Engage in manual activities: Utilize squeeze balls, pencils, clips, or any object that can fulfill the desire for tactile stimulation.

- Engage your mind: Solve crossword puzzles or Sudoku, watch a film, partake in a game, or indulge in a book.

Nicotine replacement therapy (NRT) and pharmacological interventions without nicotine.

- It is advisable to seek guidance from a healthcare professional prior to utilizing Nicotine Replacement Therapies (NRTs).

Typically, individuals with a high level of nicotine dependence may find greater effectiveness in the utilization of NRTs.

- NRTs effectively substituting cigarettes with nicotine alternatives available in:

Lozenges

Gums

Patches

Nicotine replacement therapy is designed to alleviate withdrawal symptoms. However, it is recommended to discontinue the use of NRTs after a period of three months, thereby achieving a state of complete abstinence from both nicotine-containing products, such as cigarettes, and NRTs.

- An alternative option is to consult with your physician regarding non-nicotine medications that can help alleviate cravings and alleviate withdrawal symptoms. These pharmaceuticals, namely bupropion and varenicline, are designed for a limited duration.

Recall your 'Whys'

Recall the document wherein you penned down the justifications for your desire to cease. It is imperative that you consistently keep this item in close proximity, enabling you to promptly recall your initial motivations for quitting, should the temptation to indulge arise.

Change your habits

- Hydrate yourself by increasing your intake of water. - Ensure proper hydration by consuming a higher quantity of water. - Enhance your water consumption to promote better hydration. Consuming water will diminish your appetite and maintain proper hydration.

Seek alternative solutions through verbal replacements. Ensure that your gums, carrot sticks, mints, and toothpicks are readily available at all times.

Ensure that you brush your teeth whenever you experience a craving.

- Unwind and engage in physical activity. Engage in physical exercise and seek out tranquil activities that divert your attention from smoking. Inhale deeply, exhale fully, and endeavor to acknowledge the inherent smoothness of respiration.

- Illuminate something different. - Ignite an alternate object. Instead, you have the option to ignite an incense or a candle.

Reward yourself

Each instance of successfully resisting a craving should be followed by self-reward.

Mark off the days on the calendar, beginning from the day you quit, that you have refrained from smoking.

The Month-long Challenge

Now, this marks the commencement of an enjoyable experience. Day one.

Please acquire two sheets of paper. Please transcribe the phrase "Smoking is detrimental to my health" in bold font on the initial item. Please transcribe these words onto the paper, ensuring that you encompass a maximum of ten lines. Please fold it in the manner of a cigarette and store it in a conveniently accessible location such as your pocket, wallet, purse, or dashboard.

Now, on the second sheet of paper, kindly inscribe the name of an individual who bears a deep significance in your heart, or whom you hold in the highest regard. You may also choose to designate an entity or cause that has exerted a palpable positive impact on your life—an affiliation, a particular period, an organization, an impassioned principle, or a cherished belief. The criterion is that this entity or individual must genuinely and profoundly matter to you.

Subsequent to the given name (or designated title/subject), kindly inscribe the phrase "For you."

An alternate option to the second document could be a diminutive artifact that symbolizes the topic you have recorded. It may take the form of a visual representation, such as a photograph, a symbol of significance, a religious icon, or an embodiment of your deeply-held principles and motivations. Now, proceed to place the second piece of paper or object within your preferred receptacle for discarded cigarette butts, such as your preferred ash tray, the dashboard of your automobile, or any other designated location. Please make a concerted effort to fully extinguish your cigarette or dispose of your cigarette butts directly onto the designated object whenever you smoke. It is imperative that you make every effort to engage in this activity as frequently as feasible. In the event of the flame extinguishing, such as with paper, promptly substitute it with a comparable item and proceed without delay. Please only discard your cigarette on the designated item and avoid disposing of it elsewhere.

Chapter 5: Implementation of Nicotine Replacement Therapy

Nicotine replacement therapy has been found to be a generally reliable and efficacious pharmacological intervention for smoking cessation. It alleviates withdrawal symptoms by administering controlled, minimal quantities of nicotine to the body, thereby avoiding exposure to harmful chemicals. This enables the body to fulfill its physiological desire for nicotine.

Healthcare professionals hold the belief that nicotine replacement therapy constitutes the most optimal approach for tobacco cessation. Additionally, it exhibits the fewest adverse reactions, commonly falling within the mild to moderate range for certain individuals.

Various Varieties of Nicotine Replacement Therapy

Patches

They are available for purchase without a prescription. To employ them, affix them onto your epidermis. They will administer a consistent, albeit minimal, dosage of nicotine to your system. Some potential adverse reactions may consist of skin erythema, cutaneous irritation, emesis, cephalalgia, tachycardia, insomnia, myalgia, and vertigo.

In the event that you encounter any of these adverse reactions, it is advisable to discontinue the usage of the nicotine patch and seek medical advice. You are encouraged to consider an alternative form of nicotine replacement therapy. An alternative approach would be to consider employing a nicotine patch with a reduced dosage. In the event of encountering skin irritation, it is permissible to opt for an alternative brand. If you are utilizing the 24-hour patch and encounter sleep disturbances persisting beyond a duration of four days, it is permissible to transition to the 16-hour patch.

Various strengths and varieties of nicotine patches are accessible. The 16-hour patch is suggested for individuals who engage in light to moderate smoking. It is improbable that adverse effects will manifest. Nonetheless, it is incapable of generating nicotine during the night. Hence, it may not be efficacious if your withdrawal symptoms tend to manifest during the early hours of the day.

The 24-hour transdermal patch administers a consistent nicotine dose. Therefore, it is highly suitable for individuals who encounter withdrawal symptoms during the early hours of the day. However, it is important to note that the 24-hour patch also presents a greater number of adverse effects compared to its 16-hour counterpart.

Taking into account your smoking patterns and physical composition, it is recommended to initiate the utilization of nicotine patches yielding a concentration of 15 mg to 22 mg, or those of full potency, on a daily basis throughout a duration of four weeks. Subsequently, it is advisable to utilize nicotine patches containing a dosage range of 5 mg to 14 mg or lower for an additional period of four weeks.

Ensure that you change your patch on a daily basis. It is advisable to apply it onto a surface of clean and dry skin. This region should be positioned higher than your waist and lower than your neck, for instance on your chest or upper arm. Additionally, it should possess moderate hair density. The use of nicotine patches is endorsed by the Food and Drug

Administration (FDA) for a duration of three to five months.

Lozenges

It is also possible to acquire them from a non-prescription source. Resembling hard candy in appearance, these treats can be effortlessly consumed by placing them directly in your mouth. The nicotine present within them undergoes a gradual dissolution process upon entering your oral cavity.

The strengths of nicotine lozenges that are offered include 4 mg and 2 mg options. You have the option to determine your dosage depending on the time elapsed between waking up in the morning and the moment you engage in the act of lighting a cigarette. If you have the habit of smoking within thirty minutes of waking up, the 4 mg strength is suitable for your use. If you habitually engage in smoking activities exceeding thirty minutes after awakening, the 2 mg potency is recommended for your utilization.

In an ideal scenario, it is recommended to employ a single nicotine lozenge every one to two hours throughout a period of six weeks. Subsequently, it is advisable to administer a single lozenge at intervals of two to four hours throughout the duration of the seventh to ninth weeks. It is also advisable to administer one lozenge at intervals of four to eight hours throughout the tenth to twelfth weeks.

Abstain from consuming any food or beverages for a minimum duration of fifteen minutes prior to or during the utilization of a nicotine lozenge. Please be advised that the efficacy of lozenges may be diminished by the consumption of certain beverages.

Please avoid the simultaneous usage of multiple lozenges. It is advisable to refrain from consuming a lozenge immediately following the consumption of another. Please adhere to a maximum dosage of twenty lozenges per day or five lozenges within a six-hour period. Cease the utilization of your nicotine lozenge once twelve weeks have elapsed. Should you believe it necessary to continue usage, we strongly advise seeking counsel from your physician.

Please ensure that you continue to suck on your lozenge until it fully dissolves. It is possible that you will have to engage in this activity for a duration of twenty to thirty minutes. Abstain from masticating or gnawing upon it. In lieu of that, it is advisable to carefully shift it from one side of your oral cavity to the opposite side.

The potential adverse reactions encompass gas, coughing, accelerated heartbeat, hiccups, nausea, acid reflux, aching throat, and insomnia.

Gums

They are additionally available for purchase without a prescription. They can be obtained in strengths of 2 mg and 4 mg. They exhibit characteristics akin to conventional chewing gums. In order to obtain the nicotine, it is necessary for you to masticate the substance.

Nicotine gums are fast-acting. Users have reported encountering a sensation of tingling within their oral cavity. Upon experiencing this sensation, it is advised to position the nicotine gum between the gums and cheek, allowing for the taste to dissipate before removing it. Subsequently, it is advisable to bite into it once more in order to regain the flavor. Continue to engage in this procedure for a period of twenty to thirty minutes.

Please be mindful that the consumption of beverages and edibles could potentially influence the absorption rate of nicotine. Hence, it is advisable to abstain from consuming any food or beverage for a minimum duration of fifteen minutes prior to the utilization of a nicotine gum.

When determining the appropriate dosage, it is essential to take into account whether the individual consumes a minimum of twenty-five cigarettes per day, whether they smoke within thirty minutes of waking up, and whether they experience difficulties in exercising self-control in restricted areas. If you exhibit similar symptoms, it may be necessary to administer the 4 mg dosage.

It is imperative to refrain from consuming more than twenty-four pieces of nicotine gum within a single day. Additionally, it is advisable to limit the usage of this nicotine replacement therapy product to a duration of six to twelve weeks. You are permitted to request an extension of up to a maximum duration of six months.

One can regulate the amount of nicotine intake by using nicotine gum. You are welcome to utilize it according to a designated schedule or as required. Based on the findings of researchers, adhering to a predetermined dosing schedule is deemed to be more efficacious compared to the act of chewing whenever one encounters cravings. It is recommended that one consumes one to two pieces of gum per hour.

Potential adverse effects associated with the use of nicotine gums encompass throat or mouth irritation, unfavorable aftertaste, nausea, accelerated heart rhythm, discomfort in the jaw, as well as complications relating to pre-existing dental treatments. If one is wearing dentures, there is a likelihood of adhesive adherence to the gum, potentially resulting in damage to the dentures. If you encounter any of these adverse side effects, it is imperative that you discontinue usage of the gum and seek medical advice from your physician.

Nasal Sprays

A prescription is required in order to obtain them. They can exclusively be obtained from your healthcare provider. They are available in the configuration of pump bottles. In order to obtain the nicotine, it is necessary to administer it via nasal spray. It will be absorbed quickly into your bloodstream.

The majority of users assert a preference for nasal sprays as compared to alternative nicotine replacement therapy products due to their inherent convenience and user-friendly nature. They can conveniently administer nasal nicotine spray as needed. This enables them to regulate their desires.

It is recommended that you utilize one to two doses per hour. A single dosage is comparable to a pair of sprays. It is advisable to administer a spray individually to each nostril. Upon initial usage of this product, it is recommended to administer a minimum of eight doses or sixteen sprays daily. Alternatively, it is recommended that you adhere to the guidance provided by your physician. It is advisable to refrain from exceeding a daily maximum of forty dosages or eighty sprays whenever feasible.

The Food and Drug Administration advises limiting the usage of nasal sprays to a duration of three to six months. Adverse reactions that may arise from the usage of these products encompass symptoms such as irritation in the throat or nose, increased lacrimation, coughing, sneezing, accelerated heart rate, headaches, and feelings of nervousness.

In the event that you observe these symptoms, it is advisable to discontinue the utilization of your nicotine spray. If you fail to experience improvement and your symptoms persist, it is imperative that you seek professional medical advice from your physician. May I suggest that you consider reducing the frequency of your use of the spray? You might also experience these symptoms if the dosage administered is insufficient.

Please ensure that nasal sprays are kept inaccessible to both pets and children. There may still be residual nicotine present within the empty bottles. This seemingly small amount is still enough to cause harm. Furthermore, it is advisable to refrain from coming into contact with the liquid on your skin. If the liquid comes into contact with your skin, it is imperative to promptly and thoroughly cleanse the affected area. It is advised to utilize rubber or plastic gloves while performing the cleanup of any spilled liquid.

Inhalers

In order to obtain an inhaler, it is imperative to possess a valid prescription, which can solely be obtained from a licensed medical practitioner. It is presented in the configuration of a mouthpiece that is affixed with an accompanying cartridge. In order to acquire the necessary nicotine, it is imperative to inhale through it. The nicotine will traverse through the oral cavity and be assimilated into the circulatory system.

The entirety of the cartridge can be consumed within a span of approximately twenty minutes. Furthermore, you may engage in prolonged inhalation for an extended period. It is advisable to utilize a prescribed dosage range of four to cartridges per day, progressively reducing the intake over a period of six months.

Many individuals who engage in smoking opt for nicotine inhalers due to their similarity to traditional cigarettes. Therefore, users might experience a sensation akin to smoking a cigarette whenever they utilize this device. Please be advised that these inhalers should not be confused with electronic cigarettes, as the latter have not gained approval from the FDA. On the other hand, it should be noted that nicotine inhalers are the costliest variant among the available forms of nicotine replacement therapy.

Potential adverse effects of inhalers may encompass symptoms such as coughing, irritation of the throat or mouth, nausea, nasal congestion, cephalalgia, rapid heartbeat, and feelings of unease. Typically, individuals do not encounter the side effects simultaneously. A portion of them do not encounter any sort of it, whatsoever.

Excessive consumption of nicotine can lead to specific adverse effects, including an elevated heart rate. Discontinue the usage of your inhaler in the event of this occurrence. Please exercise patience for a period of time to observe any potential improvement in your condition. Please visit your doctor to undergo a comprehensive medical examination and professional consultation. In addition, it is important to take into consideration that if your dosage is insufficient, you may encounter symptoms of withdrawal.

Additionally, it is imperative to consider that nicotine inhalers pose a significant risk to the well-being of both pets and children due to the potential retention of nicotine in used cartridges, which may result in absorption through their mucous membranes or skin. Ensure that the cartridge remains untouched and unlicked. Please promptly get in touch with Poison Control in the event of an overdose.

Prescription Medication or Pills

They aid in the reduction of the symptoms associated with nicotine withdrawal. They are devoid of nicotine. Additionally, a prescription is essential for the acquisition of these items, which are exclusively distributed by medical professionals. In addition, it is necessary to allow for the optimal absorption of the medication into your system prior to its regular use. Varenicline and Bupropion SR exemplify the prescription medications in question. In addition to mitigating withdrawal symptoms, Varenicline additionally inhibits the effects of nicotine in individuals who resume smoking.

Nicotine replacement therapy can be utilized in conjunction with specific medications to enhance their efficacy. An illustration of this could be the utilization of nicotine patches in conjunction with nicotine gums, inhalers, or nasal sprays. Furthermore, they can be employed in conjunction with Bupropion SR medications.

Given that nicotine replacement therapy solely addresses the physical manifestations, it is advisable to explore alternate approaches to address the psychological, cognitive, and affective aspects. It is advisable to consider implementing a cessation program, for example. It is advisable to incorporate a comprehensive support system into your treatment plan for an extended duration following smoking cessation. This would enhance the likelihood of maintaining a smoke-free lifestyle.

The optimal time to initiate nicotine replacement therapy (NRT) is immediately upon ceasing tobacco use. Frequently, individuals initially attempt to cease tobacco usage independently before opting to utilize nicotine replacement therapy (NRT) at least one day after commencing their quit attempt. This provides a limited probability of achieving the highest level of success, however, it should not be a deterrent to your pursuit. There exist numerous methods for cessation of the behavior and maintaining abstinence. Please be advised that it frequently requires multiple attempts.

Ensure that you carefully monitor your dosage. Although uncommon, there exists the potential for nicotine overdose. Ensure that you adhere to the instructions provided with your nicotine replacement therapy products. In the event that you encounter symptoms such as vomiting, weakness, cold perspiration, lightheadedness, rapid heartbeat, or queasiness, it is imperative that you promptly seek medical attention.

Nicotine Overdose

Nicotine replacement therapy products are equipped with explicit labels, which serve the purpose of informing users about the quantitative nicotine content they possess. They are designed to replicate the nicotine content equivalent to that found in cigarettes or tobacco products, catering to user preferences.

Please ensure that you do not exceed your required nicotine intake. Excessive intake of nicotine can pose a hazard. In addition to adhering meticulously to the instructions provided on the packaging, it is advisable to abstain from applying heat to the skin while wearing a nicotine patch. It is advisable to refrain from using a heat lamp or heating pad as they may induce heightened blood circulation, subsequently leading to an increased absorption of nicotine by the body.

Should a nicotine overdose be encountered, one may potentially encounter a range of symptoms including but not limited to: headaches, abdominal discomfort, emesis, queasiness, gastrointestinal upset, hyperactivity, unease, irregular or accelerated cardiac rhythm, diaphoresis, diminished physical strength, pallor of the oral cavity and integument, tremors, cognitive disarray, hypertensive episodes, auditory and visual disturbances, seizures, vertigo, lightheadedness, and rapid respiration.

In the event that you believe you have taken an excessive dosage, it is advisable to promptly get in touch with Poison Control in order to receive emergency assistance. Nonetheless, should you be of the opinion that you are consuming an appropriate quantity of nicotine and yet persist in encountering the aforementioned symptoms, it may be advisable to reduce your dosage and seek professional counsel from a medical practitioner.

It is essential to bear in mind that nicotine permeates both the mucous membranes and the integumentary system. Therefore, it is imperative that you take great care in storing your nicotine replacement therapy products in a secure location and ensuring their proper disposal. Ensure that they are kept inaccessible to animals and young individuals. Kindly refrain from discarding them in uncovered waste receptacles or on public thoroughfares.

Herein Lies The Segment That Has Been Eagerly Anticipated: The Benefits.

One of the most advantageous aspects of overcoming a nicotine dependency is that one can quickly experience noticeable improvements in their physical well-being. You will observe that your skin will acquire an enhanced luster previously absent, your eyes will exhibit heightened clarity and vibrancy, your breath will possess a more pleasant aroma, and your teeth will achieve a whiter appearance. Additionally, you will gradually develop an improved discernment of taste and scent, and ultimately be capable of engaging in physical exertion without experiencing breathlessness.

You are not only enhancing your personal fitness, but also positively influencing those in your immediate vicinity. It is widely acknowledged that exposure to second-hand smoke poses a significant risk, particularly to the well-being of children. Creating a smoke-free environment within your residence, workplace, or vehicle not only benefits your own well-being, but also positively impacts those in your vicinity. Therefore, it is imperative to refrain from giving up solely for one's own sake, but also for the benefit and well-being of the individuals who are intertwined in one's existence. They will express gratitude for your efforts.

Healthy mind

You will experience an enhanced ability to focus and a mindset marked by serenity and composure. You will acquire the capacity to engage in endeavors that were previously out of your reach, and it is highly probable that you will discover a marked enhancement in your personal demeanor, rendering you a more affable and agreeable individual in social contexts.

Saving money

Financial resources, monetary capital, currency! Have you considered the magnitude of your expenditures related to this compelling dependency? It is highly probable that you lack any knowledge on the topic at hand. Retrieve a writing instrument and a sheet of paper, then proceed to diligently ascertain the quantity you typically acquire within a week or day, strive to calculate the monthly expenditure in a manner that closely reflects reality. It may astound you to discover the significant monetary resources you have allocated towards ultimately compromising your physical well-being.

A highly effective incentive is to allocate that money into a designated container or a savings account. Upon the expiry of a year, you will have the capability to utilize the aforementioned funds for a substantial venture, thereby expressing gratitude towards your past self. Furthermore, this can serve as a catalyst for stimulating cravings. Develop a "desires container", wherein upon experiencing the temptation to smoke, you allocate monetary funds into said container. Here, you are effectively transforming a negative emotion into a favorable economic opportunity.

A multitude of fantastic benefits, alongside numerous others, will be eagerly awaiting your arrival upon the culmination of your arduous expedition. Maintain a steadfast awareness of this concept, persevering through both the favorable and unfavorable events and obstacles that may be encountered. Remain resilient and maintain faith in your own abilities.

Developing exemplary behavior

There has long existed a misperception that smoking is a fashionable or desirable behavior. In what way could the infusion of ailments, medical conditions, and cancerous afflictions into one's body be deemed 'fashionable' or socially desirable? By quitting smoking, you will demonstrate exemplary behavior to those in your vicinity. Upon witnessing your exceptional strength and unwavering motivation, they will be imbued with inspiration to emulate such qualities within themselves. In the near future, you will experience a boost in vitality resulting from your improved appearance and enhanced well-being, along with a gratifying sense of achievement derived from successfully adhering to your devised strategy. Demonstrate to those in your vicinity that you possess the ability to accomplish it.

Chapter 5

It is comparatively more convenient to forestall undesirable habits rather than to remediate them.
–Benjamin Franklin

A Confirmed Smoker

By the time I reached my final year of secondary education, I was consuming nearly an entire pack of cigarettes on a daily basis. Upon completing my studies, I departed from my place of residence to enlist in the Air Force. Tobacco consumption constituted a major element of the military lifestyle. The cost of a pack of cigarettes amounted to a mere seventeen cents. A package consisting of ten sets retailed for a mere $1.50.

It appeared to be the case that the act of smoking was prevalent among all individuals affiliated with the military, encompassing not only our drill instructors but also our officers. We were granted periodic smoking opportunities, provided designated receptacles for cigarette disposal within the barracks premises, and instructed in the proper technique of disassembling cigarettes in outdoor settings.

Upon the completion of my four-year service in the Air Force, I underwent a transition back into civilian life, during which time I had developed a habit of consuming nearly around forty cigarettes per day.

In the year 1964, the inaugural report issued by the United States Surgeon

General drew a correlation between smoking and the incidence of lung cancer, chronic bronchitis, and laryngeal cancer.

Shortly thereafter, the governmental authorities decreed that packages of cigarettes must bear health advisories. Despite the lack of attention from the majority, I conscientiously heeded those warnings. I possessed an inherent understanding that smoking had detrimental effects on my overall well-being.

I was aware that it was imperative for me to resign.

Upon awakening, I would declare, "Today, I shall make a concerted effort to cease my smoking habit!" Regrettably, I would succumb to the temptation of that initial morning cigarette, entertaining the thought of "just one puff." However, I failed to refrain from smoking for an entire day. Typically, by midday, I would resume smoking. I persevered in my smoking habit until I acquired a methodology that effectively suppressed my cravings and facilitated my transformation into a non-smoker.

Establishing A Network Of Support

Certain individuals exhibit a greater susceptibility to relapse compared to others, and it is of considerable value to have a dependable support system to lean on under such circumstances. A person who has achieved the goal of staying smoke-free, such as a close relative or trusted acquaintance, can offer valuable inspiration and guidance as a commendable example for your own endeavors. If you lack the presence of a mentor capable of exemplifying the ideal behavior of smoking cessation, you may instead seek solace and assistance from individuals who have triumphantly conquered their smoking habit independently. If you are still attempting to understand the intricacies of the process of quitting, it may be advantageous for you to consider joining a support group. Nevertheless, receiving assistance from a handful of individuals who comprehend the challenges you are facing can provide immense comfort during these arduous situations.

According to a study, individuals aged thirty and above who managed to quit smoking expressed that they had received considerable assistance from their social circles, most notably from their spouses, friends, and family members.

The benefits of being a member in a support group have long been acknowledged. For individuals experiencing solitude, the act of relinquishing smoking can pose greater challenges. Thus, establishing a supportive circle of individuals to lean on can serve as a valuable resource in bolstering your endeavor to quit.

It may be advisable for you to contemplate the possibility of becoming a member of an established support group or initiating the formation of a new support group, in order to alleviate the challenges you are presently facing. Seek out evening support groups as they may facilitate your ability to sustain a smoke-free lifestyle beyond dinner, subsequent to your cessation of smoking. Support groups can be organized by local healthcare institutions, via telephone, online platforms, or direct engagement with fellow participants.

A recommended course of action would be to initiate your search for local support groups in your vicinity by perusing the telephone directory. On the Internet, there exists a wide range of support groups to choose from. Additionally, you may seek information from local health organizations regarding the availability of support groups in your vicinity. To acquire guidance on identifying such a compilation, reach out to the local office of the American Lung Association.

Conveying knowledge to your support group regarding subjects such as managing anxiety, medications prescribed for anxiety, proper nutrition, methods to battle depression, aids for quitting smoking, and medications for smoking cessation can be advantageous. You can locate a support group in your vicinity by conducting a search within the yellow pages, specifically under the designated headings of "counseling," "relaxation," or "support groups."

If you choose to initiate your own support group, we recommend perusing the additional articles on this platform to gather insights and inspiration for the topics and elements you may wish to incorporate. In the event that you opt to initiate your assistance collective, you may derive inspiration from these alternate resources. Additionally, consider employing the strategies outlined in literature regarding smoking cessation to facilitate the establishment of your support network aimed at aiding your tobacco cessation efforts.

It is crucial to maintain a record of one's achievements. Commence chronicling your experiences in this journal on the day you resign from your employment. Once you have successfully completed the initial week of your cessation journey, it would be beneficial to contemplate setting a new milestone for each subsequent week until the culmination of your month-long dedication.

FACTORS CONTRIBUTING TO A RELAPSE

Similarly to you, there is a substantial number of individuals who acknowledge the drawbacks associated with smoking. Consequently, they seek an alternative to tobacco consumption. However, for individuals who are dependent on the pleasurable effects of nicotine, abstaining from smoking can appear exceedingly arduous. Your nonsmoking friend is incapable of comprehending the anguish you endure in your pursuit to abstain from smoking.

You might have endeavored to abstain, and accomplished temporary success lasting a few hours or days; however, abruptly, you find yourself unable to withstand the intense longing. It is evident that your physical well-being cannot accommodate extended intervals for cigarette breaks, leading to the realization that it is possible for you to thrive without the habit of smoking. Therefore, you promptly ignite a cigarette and commence the act of smoking. Subsequently, one becomes cognizant of the fact that their endeavor to cease smoking has not yielded any measurable achievements that can be deemed as genuine triumphs.

Considering the experience you have articulated, it is important to acknowledge that you are not in a solitary struggle. All individuals endeavoring to cease smoking experience this challenge. There exists a multitude of instances signifying this issue.

The resurgence of your smoking habit leads to a quantity of cigarettes that compensates for the ones you were unable to smoke. During this phase, your body undergoes a process of assessing the deficit of nicotine and subsequently compels you to replenish the quantity.

Remarkably, out of the individuals who make a sincere endeavor to relinquish their smoking habit, a mere 10% triumph in achieving their goal. Furthermore, a subset of individuals within this 10% may relapse into their smoking behavior. What are the key factors contributing to the difficulty in quitting smoking?

METHODS FOR MITIGATING NICOTINE DEPENDENCE

Nicotine is among the most highly addictive substances provided to individuals. The impact of nicotine becomes increasingly pronounced with higher levels of consumption.

Resolution: The key to achieving success lies within one's determination and strength of character. However, a lack of this quality is prevalent among the majority of smokers. Therefore, aside from one's own determination, supplementary assistance is highly imperative. One potential avenue for assistance entails employing nicotine patches to gradually overcome the habit of smoking. Patches play a significant role in facilitating nicotine intake while concurrently deterring the consumption of cigarettes. Alternatively, one might consider utilizing pharmaceutical interventions, such as zyban, to aid in relinquishing one's cravings for nicotine.

HOW TO CURE DEPENDANCY

Your propensity for smoking engenders a significant degree of reliance on tobacco products. Upon encountering a stressful situation, you promptly initiate a search for your pack of cigarettes.

Recommendation: Substituting your smoking behavior with a safer alternative will prove beneficial. For example, one could opt to chew gum or cinnamon sticks in lieu of consuming cigarettes. Build a new habit. Additionally, the effects of both patch and Zyban can be combined. This serves as a viable alternative for your smoking habit in the long run.

Chapter 2: The Justifications for Cessation of Smoking

There exist no justifications for you to commence the act of igniting a cigarette, while a multitude of rationales support the cessation of smoking. The sustenance of the human body relies upon the consumption of food, water, engagement in physical activity, and obtaining adequate rest; whereas, tobacco is by no means essential for its survival. Cigarettes are comprised of various chemicals, such as cyanide and nicotine, that possess the potential to harm the body through toxic effects when consumed in excessive amounts.

A positive aspect is that the human body possesses considerable intelligence. It engages in self-preservation when it perceives threats to its existence. Individuals initiating their first instance of smoking may experience a sensation akin to the scorching of their throat and lungs. Certain individuals may experience a sense of unease accompanied by vomiting tendencies when attempting to undertake the aforementioned task.

Due to its propensity to harm nearly all bodily organs and be the primary contributor to preventable mortalities, apprehension over personal well-being commonly serves as the principal motivator for individuals to discontinue smoking. Cigarette smoking, along with exposure to secondhand smoke, is responsible for a significant number of fatalities annually.

Smoking gives rise to a number of consequences that occur over time. Over a protracted period, an array of health ailments will emerge, including but not limited to stroke, cardiovascular disorders, and an assortment of cancers such as those affecting the throat, lungs, and stomach. These ailments have the potential to deprive you of your life and restrict your specific capabilities. In the near future, engaging in common physical activities, such as respiration, occupational tasks, or recreational pursuits, would become exceedingly challenging.

1. Smoking Can Cause Cancer

It is beyond question that the general population possesses awareness regarding the link between smoking and lung cancer. However, it is unfortunate that only a minority comprehends the additional peril of various other malignancies associated with smoking, including cancer of the nasal passages, oral cavity, labial regions, pharynx, renal system, urinary bladder, esophagus, gastric region, ovarian tissues, colonic structures, rectal area, and even hematological malignancies such as leukemia.

2. Smoking is associated with the development of blood vessel disorders, as well as an increased risk of experiencing strokes and heart attacks.

In contrast to individuals who do not engage in smoking, individuals who partake in this habit demonstrate an increased likelihood of experiencing mortality as a result of cardiac events. Cigarette smoking is a prominent contributor to the development of peripheral vascular disease, a condition characterized by the narrowing of the blood vessels responsible for supplying blood to the muscles in the arms and legs. Additionally, it impacts the blood vessels responsible for transporting blood to the brain, resulting in the occurrence of strokes. Smoking-induced abdominal aortic aneurysm frequently culminates in unexpected fatality as a result of the enfeeblement and rupture of the primary artery's stratified walls. Males who consistently engage in smoking habits also enhance their susceptibility to developing erectile dysfunction.

3. Smoking is associated with the development of lung diseases.

Smokers escalate their susceptibility to developing respiratory ailments, notably chronic bronchitis and emphysema. These medical conditions, known as chronic obstructive pulmonary disease or COPD, would pose significant challenges for their respiratory functioning. This condition has a tendency to exacerbate, evolving into a serious ailment. Individuals who are in their 40s have the potential to develop such illnesses; however, typically, the manifestation of symptoms reaches a critical stage before detection. Smoking is also a contributing factor to the onset of pneumonia.

4. Smoking has the potential to result in vision impairment or loss of sight.

Smoking significantly elevates the likelihood of developing macular degeneration, a prevalent cause of blindness, particularly prevalent among elderly individuals. Additionally, it contributes to the development of cataracts, which result in a loss of clarity and focus in the eye lens.

5. Association between Smoking and Additional Risks in Women and Infants

Females aged 35 and above who engage in smoking while simultaneously using oral contraceptives are at an increased risk of experiencing stroke, heart attack, as well as developing venous blood clots in the lower extremities. Additionally, they exhibit a propensity for experiencing miscarriages or giving birth to infants with lower birth weights, which may ultimately result in mortality or the development of specific physical and cognitive challenges. Sudden infant death syndrome, also known as SIDS, typically arises due to exposure to environmental tobacco smoke.

An infant may also experience the onset of asthma if a woman engages in smoking during her pregnancy. Exposure to tobacco smoke within the domicile can also contribute to the onset of otitis media, bronchitis, upper respiratory tract infections, and respiratory distress in children.

6. Smoking May Significantly Reduce Your Life Expectancy

Smoking has been found to significantly reduce life expectancy, resulting in an average reduction of 13 years for adult males and 14 years for females.

Additional factors supporting the decision to cease smoking

Bone density may also be lost because of smoking, which can lead to osteoporosis, causing the bones to become more brittle. Due to the relatively sluggish circulation of blood vessels, the passage of nutrients and oxygen to the skin is impeded. This frequently results in smokers appearing pallid and physically unfit. Additionally, smoking has been attributed to the manifestation of facial lines and the development of skin conditions, such as psoriasis.

In addition to dental discoloration, smoking cigarettes can also give rise to halitosis, a condition characterized by persistent unpleasant breath odor. When individuals engage in smoking, the odor is prone to persistently permeate their attire, hair, and even the interior of their vehicle, presenting a formidable challenge in eliminating the scent.

The act of smoking has the potential to diminish an individual's level of athletic performance. Individuals who smoke tend to refrain from engaging in competitive activities with their non-smoking acquaintances, owing to the physiological consequences associated with smoking, such as increased heart rate and respiratory difficulties. Individuals who partake in smoking exhibit reduced respiratory capacity, resulting in diminished physical activity compared to their non-smoking counterparts.

In addition to health considerations, individuals may choose to cease smoking due to the substantial financial implications associated with the habit, as the expenditure on cigarettes and tobacco products can surpass one's expectations. There are numerous additional advantageous actions and acquisitions that can be undertaken with one's financial resources. Primarily, safeguarding the wellbeing of your loved ones should provide ample justification for permanently abstaining from smoking. Please bear in mind that smoking poses serious risks to your own health as well as to the well-being of those in your vicinity.

www.ingramcontent.com/pod-product-compliance
Lightning Source LLC
Chambersburg PA
CBHW050026130526
44590CB00042B/1972